OXFORD

words & watercolours

OXFORD
words & watercolours

Selected and edited by

ELIANE WILSON

✦

Illustrations by

VALERIE PETTS

SHEPHEARD-WALWYN

Selection and Preface © Eliane Wilson, 1987
Watercolour paintings © Valerie Petts, 1987

First published in 1987 by
Shepheard-Walwyn (Publishers) Ltd,
Suite 34, 26 Charing Cross Road
London WC2H ODH

ISBN 0 85683 090 9

Printed and bound in the Netherlands by
L. van Leer & Company Ltd, Deventer.

Acknowledgements

We would like to express our gratitude to Sir Isaiah Berlin for kindly allowing us to reproduce part of the address he gave at Sir Maurice Bowra's Memorial Service in 1971, and for his encouragement.

Our grateful thanks for their kind permission to: the Classical Association for part of the Presidential Address given by Gilbert Murray in 1918; Mrs C. Day-Lewis for an extract from *The Buried Day*; Michael Hamburger for some lines from his poem 'April Day: Binsey'; and Mrs Myfanwy Thomas for extracts from Edward Thomas's *Oxford*.

For permission to include material of which they control the copyright, grateful acknowledgement is made to the following: Collins Publishers, *The Lion and the Unicorn*, by Arthur Bryant, *Letters* and *Experiment in Criticism* by C. S. Lewis, 'A Solid Man' by Luke Rigby from *C. S. Lewis at the Breakfast Table*; Constable & Co, *Soliloquies in England* by George Santayana; William Heinemann, *Zuleika Dobson* by Max Beerbohm; Longman Group, *The Life of William Morris* by J. W. Mackail; John Murray, *Collected Poems* by John Betjeman; Monro Pennefather & Co, 'Alma Mater' by Arthur Quiller-Couch; Oxford University Press, *The Complete Poems of Keith Douglas* edited by Desmond Graham; A. D. Peters & Co, *The Buried Day* by C. Day-Lewis, *Poems 1910* by Hilaire Belloc, *Undertones of War* by Edmund Blunden; Salamander Oasis Trust, 'War Poet' by Sidney Keyes; Secker and Warburg, *Sinister Street* by Compton Mackenzie; A. P. Watt Ltd, *Goodbye to all that* by Robert Graves.

Mr N. J. H. Dent most kindly allowed us to reproduce the painting on page 83. We would also like to acknowledge with thanks the courtesy of those responsible for permission to paint in the various colleges and university buildings.

And finally to our families for their patience, constructive criticism and unfailing support, our love.

Contents

Preface

When I first went to Oxford it was to discover a city I had already come to know and love through books and pictures. I am from Lausanne, where, in 1753, Edward Gibbon, sent down from Oxford for converting to Catholicism, was exiled by a shocked and angered father to study under the tutelage of a Calvinist Swiss minister. Thirty years later he returned to settle on the shores of Lac Léman and there completed the last volumes of his *Decline and Fall*. 'Such as I am, in genius, or learning, or manners, I owe my creation to Lausanne', wrote the historian in his memoirs.

Two centuries earlier, further along the lake at Geneva, Thomas Bodley — the Elizabethan who was to give Oxford a library destined to become one of the greatest in the world — had studied as a young boy when he and his family fled the religious persecution of Mary Tudor's England.

This long-lasting romance between England and Switzerland is not one-sided: for while modern English travellers inspired by Turner's watercolours, come to recapture the grandeur of the Alps and to read anew the love poems to Marguerite written by the Oxford poet, Matthew Arnold, we in Switzerland read of an England of hedgerows, orchards and gardens, and of 'that sweet city with her dreaming spires'.

In company with Valerie Petts, who lives in the shadow of St Barnabas Church (*Jude the Obscure*'s St Silas), I re-discovered the Oxford of my picture books. But Oxford is more than the physical beauty of spires, towers and bells. It embodies an ideal, the striving of Man for intellectual and spiritual truths. To portray this Oxford, I felt that my words would be inadequate, so I have selected the reflections of Oxford scholars and visitors, over the ages, linking them by a thread — the beauty of form and of human thought.

J'ay seulement faict icy un amas de fleurs estrangières, n'y ayant fourny du mien que le filet à les lier — Montaigne. (I have only gathered here a bouquet of other men's flowers, having given of mine but the thread to bind them).

Eliane Wilson
Harrow on the Hill
January 1987

For the spirit of man on beauty feedeth

Robert Bridges

Bellesitum-The Fair Place

Spirit of BEAUTY, that dost consecrate
  With thine own hues all thou dost shine upon
  Of human thought or form —

Shelley

Shadow of cloud and cantering horses race
Over the meadows where heaven and earth embrace

Michael Hamburger

FOR it is related that amongst the warlike Trojans, when with their leader Brutus they triumphantly seized upon the island, then called Albion, next Britain, and lastly England, certain Philosophers came and chose a suitable place of habitation in this island ...

Oxford Historiola, c.1375

ABOUT this time Samuel the servant of God was judge in Judea; and King Magdan had two sons; that is to say Mempricius and Malun. The younger of the two having been treacherously killed by the elder, he left the kingdom to the fratricide ... Nothing good is related of him except that he begot an honest son and heir by name Ebrancus, and built one noble city which he called from his own name *Caer-Memre*, but which afterwards, in course of time, was called *Bellisitum*, then *Caerbossa*, at length *Ridohen*, and last of all *Oxonia*, or by the Saxons *Oxenfordia*, from a certain egress out of a neighbouring ford; which name it bears to the present day. There arose here in after years an universal and noble seat of learning.

John Rous, 1486

The Cherwell, Mesopotamia

[In the year 912, Oxford entered into recorded history]

EADWEARD cyng feng to Lunden-byrig and to Oxnaforda, and to thæm landum eallum the thær to hierdon (King Edward took possession of London and of Oxford and of all the lands which owed obedience to them).

Anglo-Saxon Chronicle, 912

WHERE the Cherwell flows along with the Isis, and their divided streams make several little sweet and pleasant islands, is seated on a rising vale the most famous University of Oxford, in Saxon Oxenford, our most noble Athens, the seat of the English Muses, the prop and pillar, nay the sun, the eye, the very soul of the nation: the most celebrated fountain of wisdom and learning, from whence Religion, Letters and Good Manners, are happily diffused thro' the whole Kingdom. A delicate and most beautiful city, whether we respect the neatness of private buildings, or the stateliness of public structures, or the healthy and pleasant situation. For the plain on which it stands is walled in, as it were, with hills of wood, which keeping out on one side the pestilential south wind, on the other, the tempestuous west, admit only the purifying east, and the north that disperses all unwholesome vapours. From which delightful situation, Authors tell us it was heretofore call'd *Bellositum*.

William Camden, 1586

14

Port Meadow in flood

Nowhere else are life and art so exquisitely blended, so perfectly made into one.

Oscar Wilde

THE establishment of the great schools which bore the name of Universities was everywhere throughout Europe a special mark of the new impulse that Christendom had gained from the Crusades. A new fervour of study sprang up in the West from its contact with the more cultured East ... The long mental inactivity of feudal Europe broke up like ice before a summer's sun. Wandering teachers such as Lanfranc or Anselm crossed sea and land to spread the new power of knowledge. The same spirit of restlessness, of inquiry, of impatience with the older traditions of mankind ... crowded the roads with thousands of young scholars hurrying to the chosen seats where teachers were gathered together. A new power had sprung up in the midst of a world as yet under the rule of sheer brute force. Poor as they were, sometimes even of servile race, the wandering scholars who lectured in every cloister were hailed as 'masters' by the crowds at their feet.

At the time of the arrival of Vacarius [a leading legal scholar] Oxford stood in the first rank among English towns. Its town church of S. Martin rose from the midst of a huddled group of houses, girt in with massive walls, that lay along the dry upper ground of a low peninsula between the streams of Cherwell and the upper Thames. The ground fell gently on either side, eastward and westward, to these rivers, while on the south a sharper descent led down across swampy meadows to the city bridge. Around lay a wild forest country, the moors of Cowley and Bullingdon fringing the course of Thames, the great woods of Shotover and Bagley closing the horizon to the south and east ... From the midst of the meadows rose a mitred abbey of Austin Canons, which, with the older priory of S. Frideswide, gave the town some ecclesiastical dignity. The residence of the Norman house of the D'Oillis within its castle, the frequent visits of English kings to a palace without its walls, the presence again and again of important councils, marked its political weight within the realm ...

We know nothing of the causes which drew students and teachers within the walls of Oxford. It is possible that here as elsewhere a new teacher had quickened older educational foundations, and that the cloisters of Osney and S. Frideswide already possessed schools which burst into a larger life under the impulse of Vacarius. As yet, however, the fortunes of the University were obscured by the glories of Paris. English scholars gathered in thousands round the chairs of William of Champeaux or Abelard. The English took their place as one of the 'nations' of the French

University. John of Salisbury became famous as one of the Parisian teachers. Becket wandered to Paris from his school at Merton. But through the peaceful reign of Henry the Second Oxford was quietly increasing in numbers and repute ... At the opening of the thirteenth century Oxford was without a rival in its own country, while in European celebrity it took rank with the greatest schools of the Western world.

J. R. Green, 1874

Oxford Castle – The Mound, and The Tower from which in the winter of 1142, besieged by Stephen who had stormed Oxford, the Empress Mathilda, accompanied by three knights, made her escape. Clad in a white mantle 'she stole away & she fled' over the the snow and the frozen rivers.

Knowledge its Own End

A University is a place where the universality of the human spirit manifests itself

Einstein

Mob Quad, Merton

IT IS not the venerable appearance of University College, hallowed by the association of so many centuries in age, nor Queen's opposite, nor All Souls', nor any other of the colleges as mere buildings, that so connect them with our feelings. We must turn the mind from stone and wood to the humanity in connection with them ... It is not mere antiquity, therefore, on which our reverence for a great seminary of learning is founded ... it is the connexion of the foundation with the history of man.

J. A. Froude, 1850

THIS king [Alfred] delighted in the society of learned men, whom he knew to lead virtuous lives, and so summoned Plegmund Abp. of Canterbury, Werferth of Worcester before he was made Bishop, and Athelstan of Hereford, and Werulf of Leicester, all learned men from the kingdom of the Mercians. Also he joined with them the holy Grymbald of Flanders from the Monastery of S. Bertin, with his companions, John and Asser and John the Welshman from the Monastery of S. David's. And through their teaching he obtained knowledge of all books. At that time there were no grammarians throughout the kingdom of the West Saxons. He amongst the praiseworthy acts of his munificence, in the year 873 at the instigation of S. Neot established public schools for the several arts in Oxford; to which city on account of his special love for the scholars he granted many privileges ...

John Rous, 1486

The Master's Garden, University College
Early chroniclers who made the legendary claim that King Alfred had founded, or restored, the University, attributed the foundation of the college bearing that name, to the 'most glorious and invincible King whose memory will dwell like honey in the mouth of all'.

Logic Lane

A clerk ther was of Oxenford also,
That unto logyk hadde long ygo.
As lene was his hors as is a rake,
And he was nat right fat, I undertake,
But loked holwe, and therto soberly.
Ful thredbar was his overeste courtepy;
For he hadde geten him yet no benefice,
Ne was so worldly for to have office.
For hym was levere have at his beddes heed
Twenty bookes, clad in blak or reed,
Of Aristotle and his philosophie,
Than robes riche, or fithele, or gay sautrie.
But al be that he was a philosophre,

Yet hadde he but litel gold in cofre;
But al that he myghte of his freendes hente,
On bookes and on lernynge he it spente,
And bisily gan for the soules preye
Of hem that yaf hym wherwith to scoleye.
Of studie took he moost cure and moost heede.
Noght o word spak he moore than was neede,

And that was seyd in forme and reverence,
And short and quyk, and ful of hy sentence;
Sownynge in moral vertu was his speche,
And gladly wolde he lerne, and gladly teche.

Geoffrey Chaucer, c.1387

Study as if you were to live for ever; live as if you were to die tomorrow.

Edmund of Abingdon

St Edmund Hall, the last and longest lived of the ancient Halls, commemorates the residence in Oxford of Edmund of Abingdon, the first scholar of the University to become Archbishop of Canterbury and to be canonized as a Saint. It was said of him that: 'He fared as the olive tree that holdeth to itself the bitterness in the rind and holdeth out to others the sweetness of the oil'.

To tell you of all the varieties of arts and sciences that have anciently been presented and delivered to us by the learnedest of all ages will perhaps now, by reason of the longinguity of time, seem incredible. To tell you also of the injunctions of our old statutes, concerning the continual reading here of the three philosophical and seven liberal arts and sciences ... will also, to those that converse with the actions but of yesterday, seem riddles and chimaeras; but verily they are all so full of truth and obvious to every man's capacity, that if he doth but peep in our old statutes, or in the least give glance upon our ancient scripts, he cannot but conclude this place to be like the Aeropagus at Athens, and style it by no other name than *Vicus Minervalis*. Here, had we lived in those days, we might have beheld with what great emulation our old philosophers would open their packs of literature (as I may say) to their hungry auditors. Here also, each order in our University at their first coming and plantation, would with great pride endeavour to blazon their parts, and give the world approbation of their profound knowledge and deep discoveries of those muffled-up secrets of theology and philosophy.

Anthony Wood, 1661-6

Merton Street and the house of Anthony Wood

I HAD never been in Merton Gardens before. They are very beautiful and the famous Terrace Walk upon the old city walls and the lime avenue are most delightful. The soft green sunny air was filled with the cooing of doves and the chiming of innumerable bells. It was a beautiful peaceful spot where abode an atmosphere of calm and happy security and the dewy garden was filled with a sweet green gloom as we loitered along the celebrated Terrace Walk, looking on one hand from the ancient City walls upon Merton Meadows and the Cathedral spire rising from the grey clustered buildings of Christ Church and the noble elms of the Broad Walk which hid from us the barges and the gay river, and delighting on the other side in the picturesque grey sharp gables of Merton College half veiled by the lime avenue rising from the green soft lawns and reposing in the silence and beauty and retirement of the shady happy garden. We suddenly became aware that the peace of this paradise was being disturbed by the voices and laughter and trampling of a company of people and immediately there came into sight a master and a bachelor of arts in caps and gowns carrying a ladder on their shoulders assisted by several men, and attended by a number of parish boys. Every member of the company bore in his hand a long white peeled willow wand with which they were noisily beating and thrashing the old City walls and the Terrace Walk. 'They are beating the bounds', exclaimed Mayhew. The master of arts was Knox, the Vicar of the Merton living and parish of St John the Baptist, the bachelor of arts was one of the Fellows of Merton and the men in attendance were Churchwardens, clerks, sidesmen and parish authorities. The ladder was let down over the city walls at two places where the walls were crossed by the parish bounds and at certain important points which it was desired that the boys should keep in mind they were made to scramble for sweetmeats.

We determined to follow the procession and see the end. We came down into Deadman's Walk and then passed up a flight of steps and through an iron gate into Corpus Gardens. Here we were stopped by a gate of which the key could not be found for some time. In this quarter the parish boundary ran through an outhouse where used to be an ancient wheel for raising water. In this outhouse a cross was scratched upon a particular stone to mark where the boundary passed through the wall. By this time the missing key had been found and we found ourselves in the private garden of the President of Corpus, Matthias Wilson. It seemed to be an ancient custom here that those who beat the bounds should be regaled with bread, cheese and ale from the private buttery of the President of Corpus. Accordingly we gathered under an old archway while the customary dole was handed out to us over the buttery hatch ...

The bounds now led us through an outer court where the parish boys were liberally splashed with cold water by undergraduates from the windows of the upper rooms. Eventually we emerged close by Canterbury Gate and went in to Oriel. Here there was a grand uproar in the quadrangle, the men threw out to the boys old hats (which were immediately used as footballs), biscuits were also thrown out and hot coppers, and the quadrangle echoed with shouting and laughter and the whole place was filled with uproar, scramble, and general licence and confusion. Knox could scarcely get his boys under control again, but at length we went up the hall steps, down through the cloisters into the kitchen precincts where there was a Hogarthian scene and a laughable scrimmage with the young flat-white-capped cooks that might have furnished a picture for the Idle Apprentice. The procession passed next up Oriel Lane and here we left them.

Francis Kilvert, 1876

IF the writer should at all appear to have induced any of his readers to pay a more ready attention to the wonders of the Creation, too frequently overlooked as common occurrences ... his purpose will be fully answered.

... I cannot agree with those persons that assert that the swallow kind disappear some and some gradually, as they come, for the bulk of them seem to withdraw at once: only some stragglers stay behind a long while, and do never, leave this island. Swallows seem to lay themselves up, and to come forth in a warm day ... after they have disappeared for weeks. For a very respectable gentleman assured me that, as he was walking with some friends under Merton-wall on a remarkably hot noon, either in the last week in December or the first week in January, he espied three or four swallows huddled together on the moulding of one of the windows of that college. I have frequently remarked that swallows are seen later at Oxford than elsewhere: is it owing to the vast massy buildings of that place, to the many waters round it, or to what else?

Gilbert White, 1789

Give me my scallop-shell of quiet,
My staff of Faith to walk upon,
My script of joy, immortal diet,
My bottle of salvation,
My gown of glory, hope's true gage,
And thus I'll take my pilgrimage.

Walter Ralegh, 1604

Oriel College, Middle Quad

THE capture of Constantinople by the Turks, and the flight of its Greek scholars to the shores of Italy, opened anew the science and literature of the older world at the very hour when the intellectual energy of the Middle Ages had sunk into exhaustion. The exiled Greek scholars were welcomed in Italy, and Florence, so long the home of freedom and of art, became the home of an intellectual revival. The poetry of Homer, the drama of Sophocles, the philosophy of Aristotle and of Plato woke again to life . . . Foreign scholars soon flocked over the Alps to learn Greek, the key of the new knowledge, from the Florentine teachers. Grocyn, a fellow of New College, was perhaps the first Englishman who studied under the Greek exile, Chalcondylas; and the Greek lectures which he delivered in Oxford on his return mark the opening of a new period in our history. Physical as well as literary activity awoke with the re-discovery of the

View from Christ Church Meadows

teachers of Greece, and the continuous progress of English science may be dated from the day when Linacre, another Oxford student, returned from the lectures of the Florentine Politian to revive the older tradition of medicine by his translation of Galen.

But from the first it was manifest that the revival of letters would take a tone in England very different from the tone it had taken in Italy, a tone less literary, less largely human, but more moral, more religious, more practical in its bearings both upon society and politics.

The awakening of a rational Christianity ... began with the Italian studies of John Colet ... He came back to Oxford utterly untouched by the Platonic mysticism or the semi-serious infidelity which characterized the group of scholars round Lorenzo the Magnificent. He was hardly more influenced by their literary enthusiasm. The knowledge of Greek seems to

Valerie Petts

have had one almost exclusive end for him, and this was a religious end . . . Severe as was the outer life of the new teacher . . . his lively conversation, his frank simplicity, the purity and nobleness of his life . . . endeared him to a group of scholars among whom Erasmus and Thomas More stood in the foremost rank.

At the time of Colet's return from Italy Erasmus was young and comparatively unknown . . . It was in despair of reaching Italy that the young scholar made his way to Oxford, as the one place on this side of the Alps where he would be enabled through the teaching of Grocyn to acquire a knowledge of Greek. But he had no sooner arrived there than all feeling of regret vanished away. 'I have found in Oxford', he writes, 'so much polish and learning that now I hardly care about going to Italy at all . . . When I listen to my friend Colet it seems like listening to Plato himself. Who does not wonder at the wide range of Grocyn's knowledge? What can be more searching, deep, and refined than the judgement of Linacre? When did Nature mould a temper more gentle, endearing, and happy than the temper of Thomas More?'

. . . the group of scholars who represented the New Learning in England still remained a little one through the reign of Henry the Seventh. But a 'New Order', to use their own enthusiastic term, dawned on them with the accession of his son, Henry the Eighth . . . His sympathies were known to be heartily with the New Learning; for Henry was not only himself a fair scholar, but even in boyhood had roused by his wit and attainments the wonder of Erasmus . . .

At Oxford the Revival met with fierce opposition. The contest took the form of boyish frays, in which the young partizans and opponents of the New Learning, took sides as Greeks and Trojans. The King himself had to summon one of its fiercest enemies to Woodstock, and to impose silence on the tirades which were delivered from the University pulpit. The preacher alleged that he was carried away by the Spirit. 'Yes', retorted the King 'by the spirit, not of wisdom, but of folly'. But even at Oxford the contest was soon at an end.

Fox, Bishop of Winchester, established the first Greek lecture, there in his new college of Corpus Christi. 'The students', wrote an eye-witness, 'rush to Greek letters, they endure watching, fasting, toil, and hunger in the pursuit of them'.

The work was crowned at last by the munificent foundation of Cardinal College [Christ Church] to share in whose teaching Wolsey invited the most eminent of the living scholars of Europe.

J. R. Green, 1874

> This cardinal,
> Though from a humble stock, undoubtedly
> Was fashion'd to much honour from his cradle.
> He was a scholar, and a ripe and good one;
> Exceeding wise, fair-spoken, and persuading:
> Lofty and sour to them that lov'd him not;
> But, to those men that sought him, sweet as
>   summer.
> And though he were unsatisfied in getting,
> (Which was a sin) yet in bestowing, madam,
> He was most princely: ever witness for him
> Those twins of learning, that he rais'd in you,
> Ipswich, and Oxford! one of which fell with him,
> Unwilling to outlive the good that did it;
> The other, though unfinish'd, yet so famous,
> So excellent in art, and still so rising,
> That Christendom shall ever speak his virtue.

William Shakespeare, 1612

31

The fan-vaulting at Christ Church

ALL our colleges — though some of them are simply designed — are yet richly built, never pinchingly. Pieces of princely costliness, every here and there, mingle among the simplicities or severities of the student's life. What practical need, for instance, have we at Christ Church of the beautiful fan-vaulting under which we ascend to dine? We might have as easily achieved the eminence of our banquets under a plain vault. What need have the readers in the Bodleian of the ribbed traceries which decorate the external walls? Yet, which of those readers would not think that learning was insulted by their removal? . . . In these and also other regarded and pleasant portions of our colleges, we find always a wealthy and worthy completion of all appointed features, which I believe is not without strong, though untraced effect, on the minds of the younger scholars, giving them respect for the branches of learning which those buildings are intended to honour, and increasing, in a certain degree, that sense of the value of delicacy and accuracy which is the first condition of advance in those branches of learning themselves.

John Ruskin, 1870

THE process of living seems to consist in coming to realize truths so ancient and simple that, if stated, they sound like barren platitudes. They cannot sound otherwise to those who have not had the relevant experience; that is why there is no real teaching of such truths possible and every generation starts from scratch ...

C. S. Lewis, 1939

MR. Lewis was no academician in the narrow sense. In appearance and manner, he was hale and hearty — a big man, ruddy of complexion, rarely separated from his pipe in tutorials and often with a mug of beer. He dressed in tweeds and flannels verging on the shabby, and I have a strangely detailed memory of a tattered pair of carpet slippers. His appearance both reflected and belied the man within. It reflected the warmth and geniality of the man — a true kindness that soon put a green and overawed freshman at his ease; it reflected a straightforward and down-to-earth condemnation of the pseudo — the shoddy and the insincere.

On the other hand, it belied the depth of his learning that I was early to witness; it belied, too, the poetic and personal sensitivity that was evident in his perceptive enthusiasm and appreciation of beauty in words; in particular I think it belied what I was dimly aware of at the time, the sensitive and lonesome man of vision. What stands out in my memory is the warmth of the man. He was always welcoming and showed total interest and concern. The startling contrast between his achievement in the world of literature and my mediocre promise did not open a gulf; he was the true master, the true teacher. He shared his appreciation and enthusiasm and thereby instilled confidence and demanded effort; to some extent he was a hard taskmaster but that seemed good ...

Before I went up to Oxford, a warm and wise counselor with perhaps a sombre cast of mind said to me: 'The university will be for you a lesson in humility. What you may learn of your subject will not compare in value with what you learn from being in contact with minds immeasurably more gifted than your own; you will marvel at the potential of the human mind.' Mr. Lewis provided me with my first and most abiding lesson in this sphere.

Luke Rigby, 1974

Yes, I do feel the old Magdalen years to have been a v. important period in both our lives. More generally, I feel the whole of one's youth to be immensely important and even of immense length. The gradual *reading* of one's own life, seeing a pattern emerge, is a great illumination at our age.

C. S. Lewis, 1956

Magdalen Cloisters

ON May Morning, when the choir-boys of St Mary's hymned the rising sun, Michael was able for the first time to behold the visible expression of his own mental image of Oxford's completeness, to pierce in one dazzling moment of assurance the cloudy and elusive concepts which had restlessly gathered and resolved themselves in beautiful obscurity about his mind. He was granted on that occasion to hold the city, as it were, imprisoned in a crystal globe, and by the intensity of his evocation to recognise perfectly that uncapturable quintessence of human desire and human vision so supremely displayed through the merely outward glory of its repository ...

Slowly, however, the sky lightened: slowly the cold hues and blushes of the sun's youth, that stood as symbol for so much here in St Mary's, made of the east one great shell of lucent colour. The grey stones of the college lost the mysterious outlines of dawn and sharpened slowly to a rose-warmed vitality. The choir-boys gathered like twittering birds at the base of the tower: energetic visitors came half shyly through the portal that was to give such a sense of time's rejuvenation as never before had they deemed possible: dons came hurrying like great black birds in the gathering light: and at last the tired revellers ... equipped in cap and gown, went scrambling and laughing up the winding stairs to the top.

For Michael the moment of waiting for the first shaft of the sun was scarcely to be endured: the vision of the city below was almost too poignant during the hush of expectancy that preceded the declaration of worship. Then flashed a silver beam in the east: the massed choir-boys with one accord opened their mouths and sang just exactly, Michael said to himself, like the morning stars. The rising sun sent ray upon ray lancing over the roofs of the outspread city until with all its spires and towers, with all its domes and houses and still, unpopulous streets, it sparkled like the sea. The hymn was sung: the choir-boys twittered again like sparrows and, bowing their greetings to one another, the dons cawed gravely like rooks. The bells incredibly loud here on the tower's top crashed out so ardently that every stone seemed to nod in time as the tower trembled and swayed backwards and forwards while the sun mounted into the day.

Compton Mackenzie, 1914

Magdalen Tower from the Botanic Gardens

AMONGST ye severall famous structures & curiosities wherewith ye flourishing Univerisity of Oxford is enriched, that of ye Publick Physick Garden deserves not ye last place, being a matter of great use & ornament, prouving serviceable not only to all Physitians, Apothecaryes, and those who are more immediately concerned in the practise of Physick, but to persons of all qualities serving to help ye diseased and for ye delight & pleasure of those of perfect health, containing therein 3000 severall sorts of plants for ye honor of our nation and Universitie & service of ye Commonwealth . . .

Thomas Baskerville, 1677

The Nun's Garden, The Queen's College

FOR her inner secret heart remains as beautiful as ever. One can pass out of the petrol-scented, piston-banging barbarism of the twentieth century High into the green serenity and quietude of College garden and quadrangle, flanked by buildings rich with the patina of centuries. To sit on some hallowed lawn in the long, quiet dusk of May, to dine off ancient mahogany and silver in Hawksmoor's cool and temperate English baroque, to stand amid whispering ghosts on the long, cold floor of a noble library, with the darkening twilight flooding through the great traceried windows, to see the dome of the Camera glowing rose-like against the blue of night or the eagle-topped glory of a Wren façade floodlit for a College play; to walk under the ancient city wall with a friend in darkness, while the flowers of the limes give out their first fugitive scent, to lie listening to those magical bells which hour by hour have made music for half a thousand years, to rise from one's bed and gaze on the enchanted scene — moonlit garden, tower, dome, spire, pinnacle and lichened wall — and see the ghost of an English Creseid, as Chaucer pictured her, tiptoeing down the mediaeval stone steps to the waiting lawn and the dark, blossoming trees below; such are the enchantments this magical city of learning still offers ...

Arthur Bryant, 1969

As for recreation, if a man be wearied with over-much study (for study is a wearinesse to the Flesh as Solomon by experience can tell you) there is no better place in the world to recreate himself than a Garden, there being no sence but may be delighted therein.

If his sight be obfuscated and dull, as it may easily be, with continually poring, there is no better way to relieve it, than to view the pleasant greenesse of Herbes, which is the way that Painters use, when they have almost spent their sight by their most earnest contemplation of brighter objects: neither doe they only feed the Eyes, but comfort the wearied Braine with fragrant smells which yield a certaine kind of nourishment . . .

Dr. Pinck, late Warden of New College in Oxon, whereof I was once a Member (whose memory I very much honour) was a very learned Man, and well versed in Physic, and truly he would rise very betimes in the morning . . . and going into his Garden, he would take a Mattock or Spade, digging there an houre or two, which he found very advantageous to his health.

William Coles, 1656

[During the Civil War, when the tower and cloisters of New College were turned into a magazine, the Royalist Warden supervised the drilling of the volunteers in the front quadrangle.]

When first for Oxford, fully there intent
To study learned Sciences I went,
Instead of Logicke, Physicke, School Converse,
I did attend the armed Troops of Mars;
Instead of Books, I, Sword, Horse, Pistols, bought,
And on the Field I for Degrees then fought . . .

A. C., 1662

New College Gardens

THE gardens of New College are indescribably beautiful ... lawns of richest green and softest velvet grass, shadowed over by ancient trees that have lived a quiet life here for centuries and have been nursed and tended with such care, and so sheltered from rude winds that certainly they must have been the happiest of all trees. Such a sweet, quiet, sacred, stately seclusion so age-long as this has been and I hope will continue to be – cannot exist anywhere else ...

Nathaniel Hawthorne, 1856

THE flat roof of the Theatre has no pillars to support it, being kept up with braces and screws, and whose main beams are made up of several pieces of timber, from sidewall to sidewall 80 feet one way, and 70 the other, whose lockages are in some respects not to be paralleled in the world.

John Pointer, 1749

The Broad with the Sheldonian designed by Christopher Wren and the Clarendon Building built with the proceeds from the perpetual copyright in Clarendon's 'History of the Rebellion'.

IF the celebrating the memory of eminent and extraordinary persons, and transmitting their great virtues for the imitation of posterity, be one of the principal ends and duties of history, it will not be thought impertinent in this place to remember a loss which no time will suffer to be forgotten, and no success or good fortune could repair. In this unhappy battle was slain the Lord Viscount Falkland: a person of such prodigious parts of learning and knowledge, of that inimitable sweetness and delight in conversation, of so flowing and obliging a humanity and goodness to mankind, and of that primitive simplicity and integrity of life, that if there were no other brand upon this odious and accursed civil war than that single loss, it must be most infamous and execrable to all posterity.

Clarendon, 1646

HIS house where he usually resided (Tew, or Burford, in Oxfordshire), being within ten or twelve miles of the University, looked like the university itself, by the company that was always found there. There were Dr. Sheldon, Dr. Morley, Dr. Hammond, Dr. Earle, Mr. Chillingworth, and indeed all men of eminent parts and faculties in Oxford, besides those who resorted thither from London; who all found their lodgings there, as ready as in the colleges; nor did the lord of the house know of their coming or going, nor who were in his house, till he came to dinner, or supper where all still met; otherwise, there was no troublesome ceremony or constraint, to forbid men to come to the house, or make them weary of staying there; so that many came thither to study in a better air, finding all the books they could desire in his library, and all the persons together, whose company they could wish, and not find in any other society.

Clarendon, 1667

[Worcester College has its origins in a Benedictine Foundation, the first House of Study of a Monastic Order to be established in Oxford, under the name of Gloucester College.]

AT what time then this place was founded for the monks of Glocester was on St. John the Evangelists' day anno 1283; there being present (I meane in St. Peter's Abby at Glocester) Reginald the reverend abbat and covent therof and John Giffard the founder, who willingly consenting therunto, instituted it a nursery and mansion place solely for them, and setled therin 13 monks of the same place to be allwayes chosen successively from Glocester Abbey to his college at Oxon. They being then setled here and for some yeares occupying themselves in all manner of philosophicall and theologicall exercises took their degrees as other academians did.

Thus wee find this place at first possessed only by the monks of Glocester and by them solely inhabited, till at length the rest of other abbyes of this Order that were destitute of such habitations in this University, considering how advantagious it would be if they could obtaine the like, did humbly desire the abbat and covent of St. Peter's in Glocester that they would permit an enlargment to be added to their buildings for the entertainment of monks of severall abbyes of the same Order.

Which they permitting, applied themselves to the founder, John Giffard, for an addition of land to erect the same building on, as alsoe for an enlargment of walkes ... upon which gift, ... built severall lodgings here ... and divided (though all for the most part adjoyning to each other) by particular roofes, partitions, and various formes of structure: and knowne from each other, like soe many colonies and tribes (though one at once inhabited by several abbyes) by armes and rebuses that are depicted and cutt in stone over each doore.

Anthony Wood, 1661

The Cottages, Worcester College, the only remaining part of Gloucester College.

St John's College

'... and God's everlasting blessing be upon that place

and that society for ever' wrote Archbishop Laud, one of Oxford's greatest benefactors, in his last will, while a prisoner in the Tower of London. Impeached of high treason by the Long Parliament, he was beheaded in 1645.

WE repaired in turn to a series of gardens and spent long hours sitting in their greenest places. They struck us as the fairest things in England and the ripest and sweetest fruit of the English system. Locked in their antique verdure, guarded, as in the case of New College, by gentle battlements of silver-grey, outshouldering the matted leafage of undisseverable plants, filled with nightingales and memories, a sort of chorus of tradition; with vaguely-generous youths sprawling bookishly on the turf as if to spare it the injury of their boot-heels, and with the great conservative college countenance appealing gravely from the restless outer world, they seem places to lie down on the grass in for ever, in the happy faith that life is all a green old English garden and time an endless summer afternoon. This charmed seclusion was especially grateful to my friend, and his sense of it reached its climax, I remember, on one of the last of such occasions and while we sat in fascinated *flânerie* over against the sturdy back of Saint John's ... 'Isn'it all a delightful lie?' he wanted to know. 'Mightn't one fancy this the very central point of the world's heart, where all the echoes of the general life arrive but to falter and die? Doesn't one feel the air just thick with arrested voices?'

Henry James, 1875

July 12, 1654: We went to St. John's, saw the library and the two skeletons which are finely cleans'd and put together; observable is here also the store of mathematical instruments, cheifly given by the late Archbishop Laud, who built here an handsome quadrangle ... Hence we went to the Physick Garden, where the sensitiver plant was shew'd us for a greate wonder. There grew canes, olive-trees, rhubarb, but no extraordinary curiosities, besides very good fruit, which, when the ladys had tasted, we returned in our coach to our lodgings.

July 13: We all din'd at that most obliging and universally curious Dr. Wilkins's at Wadham College. He was the first who shew'd me the transparent apiaries, which he had built like castles and palaces, and so order'd them one upon another, as to take the hony without destroying the bees. These were adorn'd with a variety of dials, little statues, vanes &c ... He had also contriv'd an hollow statue, which gave a voice and utter'd words by a long conceal'd pipe that went to its mouth, whilst one speaks through it at a good distance. He had, above in his lodgings and gallery, variety of shadows, dyals, perspectives, and many other artificial, mathematical and magical curiosities, a way-wiser, a thermometer, a monstrous magnet, conic and other sections, a ballance on a demi-circle most of them of his owne, and that prodigious young scholar Mr. Chr. Wren, who presented me with a piece of white marble, which he had stain'd with a lively red, very deepe, as beautiful as if it had been natural....

October 24, 1664: I went to visite Mr Boyle (now here), whom I found with Dr. Wallis, and Dr. Christopher Wren in the Tower of the Scholes, with an inverted tube or telescope, observing the discus of the sunn for the passing of Mercury that day before it but the latitude was so great that nothing appear'd — so we went to see the rarities in the Library, where the keepers shew'd me my name among the benefactors. They have a cabinet of some medails, and pictures of the muscular parts of a man's body ...

John Evelyn

When we build,
let us think that
we build forever ...

John Ruskin

The University Museum

IT has taken some centuries from the epoch of Roger Bacon, followed here by Boyle, Harvey, Linacre and Sydenham, besides nearly 200 years of unbroken publication of the Royal Society's Transactions, to persuade this great English University to engraft, as a substantial part of the education of her youth, any knowledge of the great material design of which the Supreme Master-Worker has made us a constituent part. 'The study of mankind', indeed, was 'Man'; but in Oxford it was Man viewed apart from all those external circumstances and conditions by which his probation on earth was made by his Maker possible, and through whose agency, for good and evil, his life here, and preparation for life hereafter, were ordained.

Seeing them, all these things, many here in Oxford, not so much by concert, as by that strange unanimity which comes to some subjects in the fulness of their time, felt as by an instinct, that they might not rest until means for rightly studying what is vouchsafed for man to know of this universe were accorded to the youth committed to their care, and to themselves. From such causes, and from so deep convictions, has arisen the Oxford Museum.

Henry W. Acland, 1859

'THERE used to be much snapdragon growing on the walls opposite my freshman's rooms there [Trinity] and I had for years taken it as the emblem of my own perpetual residence, even unto death, in my University,' wrote Cardinal Newman, the soul of the Oxford Movement.

THE scene of this new Movement was as like as it could be in our modern world to a Greek πόλις, or an Italian self-centred city of the Middle Ages. Oxford stood by itself in its meadows by the rivers, having its relations with all England, but, like its sister at Cambridge, living a life of its own, unlike that of any other spot in England, with its privileged powers, and exemptions from the general law, with its special mode of government and police, its usages and tastes and traditions, and even costume, which the rest of England looked at from the outside, much interested but much puzzled, or knew only by transient visits. And Oxford was as proud and jealous of its own ways as Athens or Florence; and like them it had its quaint fashions of polity; its democratic Convocation and its oligarchy; its social ranks; its discipline, severe in theory and often lax in fact; its self-governed bodies and corporations within itself; its faculties and colleges, like the guilds and 'arts' of Florence; its internal rivalries and discords; its 'sets' and factions. Like these, too, it professed a special recognition of the supremacy of religion; it claimed to be a home of worship and religious training, *Dominus illuminatio mea* ... It was a small sphere, but it was a conspicuous one; for there was much strong and energetic character, brought out by the aims and conditions of University life; and though moving in a separate orbit, the influence of the famous place over the outside England, though imperfectly understood, was recognized and great.

R. W. Church, 1891

IF such was the general aspect of Oxford society at that time, where was the centre and soul from which so mighty a power emanated? It lay, and had for some years lain, mainly in one man – a man in many ways the most remarkable that England has seen during this century ... John Henry Newman. The influence he had gained, apparently without setting himself to seek it, was something altogether unlike anything else in our time. A mysterious veneration had by degrees gathered round him, till now it was almost as though some Ambrose or Augustine of elder ages had reappeared ...

J. C. Shairp, 1872

THE Garden Quadrangle at Balliol is where one walks at night and listens to the wind in the trees, and weaves the stars into the web of one's thoughts; where one gazes from the pale inhuman moon to the ruddy light of the windows, and hears broken notes of music and laughter . . . The life here is very sweet and full of joy; at Oxford, after all, one's ideal of happy life is nearer being realised than anywhere else; I mean the ideal of gentle, equable, intellectual intercourse, with something of a prophetic glow about it, glancing brightly into the future, yet always embalming itself in the memory as a resting-place for the soul in a future time that may be dark and troubled after all . . .

Arnold Toynbee, 1884

Trinity College from The Fellows' Garden, Balliol – and Oscar (the tortoise)

Sculpture of Maurice Bowra, Wadham College

MAURICE BOWRA, scholar, critic and administrator, the greatest English wit of his day, was, above all, a generous and warm-hearted man, whose powerful personality transformed the lives and outlook of many who came under his wide and life-giving influence . . . Bowra loved life in all its manifestations. He loved the sun, the sea, warmth, light, and hated cold and darkness, physical, intellectual, moral, political. All his life he liked freedom, individuality, independence, and detested everything that seemed to him to cramp and constrict the forces of human vitality, no matter what spiritual achievements such self-mortifying asceticism might have to its credit ...

Consequently he had little sympathy for those who recoiled from the forces of life — cautious, calculating conformists, or those who seemed to him prigs or prudes who winced at high vitality or passion, and were too easily shocked by vehemence and candour ...

Bowra was a major liberating force: the free range of his talk about art, personalities, poetry, civilisations, private life, his disregard of accepted rules, his passionate praise of friends and unbridled denunciation of enemies, produced an intoxicating effect.

Isaiah Berlin, 1971

RESTLESSNESS is the leitmotiv of my Oxford memories ... Such unrest, with its temporary disorientation, is to be expected at the turn from adolescence to manhood. But at Oxford it was heightened by intellectual ferment: the impact of a mature society upon the more or less unsophisticated freshman, the intoxication of larger intercourse with brilliant minds, living and dead, the heady, home-brewed ideas to which we treated one another ...

Ideas were the sirens that sang to us, seducing our virgin minds with the charms of the forbidden, the paradoxical or the shamelessly abstract: like adventurers on unknown seas, we lived for a few years in a world and weather of discovery, as we voyaged enchantedly among the eternal truisms.

It was ourselves, of course, that we were discovering thus — the range and quality and hidden resources of our minds; and we were fortunate enough to be doing so at a period of history which, though deeply disturbed, did not occlude the future, in a place where self-discovery was still valued as a cardinal aim of education ... At Oxford the maxim I had first learnt at school, 'Know thyself', took on richer meaning and more urgent importance, linking itself in my mind with ... intellectual honesty.

C. Day-Lewis, 1960

MY own eyes are not enough for me; I will see through those of others. Reality, even seen through the eyes of many, is not enough ... Literary experience heals the wound, without undermining the privilege of individuality. There are mass emotions which heal the wound; but they destroy the privilege. In them our separate selves are pooled and we sink back into subindividuality. But in reading great literature I become a thousand men and yet remain myself. Like the night sky in the Greek poem, I see with a myriad eyes, but it is still I who see. Here, as in worship, in love, in moral action, and in knowing, I transcend myself; and am never more myself than when I do.

C. S. Lewis, 1961

I SPEND all my mornings in the Bodleian ... If only one could smoke and if only there were upholstered chairs, this would be one of the most delightful places in the world. I sit in 'Duke Humphrey's Library', the oldest part, a Fifteenth Century building with a very beautiful wooden painted ceiling above me and a little mullioned window on my left hand through which I look down on the garden of Exeter, where these mornings I see the sudden squalls of wind and rain driving the first blossoms off the fruit trees and snowing the lawn with them. At the bottom of the room the gilt bust of Charles I, presented by Laud, faces the gilt bust of Strafford – poor Strafford. The library itself – I mean the books – is mostly in a labyrinth of cellars under the neighbouring squares. This room however is full of books which stand in little cases at right angles to the wall, so that between each pair there is a kind of little 'box' — in the public-house sense of the word – and in these boxes one sits and reads. By a merciful provision, however many books you send for, they will be left on your chosen table at night for you to resume work next morning; so that one gradually accumulates a pile as comfortably as in one's own room. There is not, as in modern libraries, a forbidding framed notice to shriek 'Silence'; on the contrary the more moderate request, 'Talk little and tread lightly'. There is indeed always a faint murmur going on of semi-whispered conversations in the neighbouring boxes. It disturbs no one. I rather like to hear the hum of the hive ...

Positively the only drawback is that beauty, antiquity and overheating weave a spell much more suited to dreaming than to working ...

C. S. Lewis, 1928

54

The Divinity School, Bodleian Library

The chiefest wonder in Oxford is a faire Divinitie Schoole with church windows and over it the fairest librarie.

Roger Wilbraham

THE Oxford in which Morris and Burne-Jones began their residence at the end of January, 1853, was still in all its main aspect a mediaeval city, and the name (in Morris's own beautiful words) roused, as it might have done at any time within the four centuries then ended, 'a vision of grey-roofed houses and a long winding street, and the sound of many bells' . . .

Morris and Burne-Jones made each other's acquaintance within the first two or three days of their first term. At first sight each found in the other a kindred and complemental spirit. Within a week they were inseparable friends with that complete and unreserved friendship which is the greatest of all the privileges that Oxford life has to bestow . . . In the Michaelmas term of 1853 they moved into rooms in college. Morris's rooms were in the little quadrangle affectionately known among Exeter men as Hell Quad, with all windows overlooking the small but beautiful Fellows' garden, the immense chestnut tree that overspreads Brasenose Lane, and the grey masses of the Bodleian Library . . . The two read together omnivorously . . . Ruskin became for both of them a hero and a prophet . . . The famous chapter 'Of the Nature of Gothic' [The Stones of Venice] long afterwards lovingly reprinted by Morris as one of the earliest productions of the Kelmscott Press, was a new gospel and a fixed creed.

J. W. Mackail, 1899

I BEGAN printing books with the hope of producing some which would have a definite claim to beauty, while at the same time they should be easy to read and should not dazzle the eye, or trouble the intellect of the reader by eccentricity of form in the letters. I have always been a great admirer of the calligraphy of the Middle Ages, and of the earlier printing which took its place. As to the fifteenth century books, I had noticed that they were always beautiful by force of the mere typography, even without the added ornament, with which many of them are so lavishly supplied. And it was the essence of my undertaking to produce books which it would be a pleasure to look upon as pieces of printing and arrangement of type. Looking at my adventure from this point of view then, I found I had to consider chiefly the following things: the paper, the form of the type, the relative spacing of the letters, the words, and the lines; and lastly the position of the printed matter on the page . . .

William Morris, 1891

The Fellows' Garden, Exeter College. The curve of the path was designed in accordance with Hogarth's leading principle of beauty. It follows the same serpentine line as drawn on the palette in the artist's self-portrait.

Brasenose College and the dome of the Radcliffe Camera

EVERY moment some form grows perfect in hand or face; some tone on the hills or sea is choicer than the rest; some mood of passion or insight or intellectual excitement is irresistibly real and attractive for us for that moment only. Not the fruit of experience but experience itself is the end. A counted number of pulses only is given to us of a variegated, dramatic life. How may we see in them all that is to be seen in them by the finest senses? How can we pass most swiftly from point to point, and be present always at the focus where the greatest number of vital forces unite in their purest energy?

To burn always with this hard gem-like flame, to maintain this ecstasy, is success in life ... While all melts under our feet, we may well catch at any exquisite passion, or any contribution to knowledge that seems by a lifted horizon to set the spirit free for a moment, or any stirring of the senses, strange dyes, strange flowers and curious odours, or work of the artist's hands, or the face of one's friend ...

Walter Pater, 1873

The Ey's confind, the Body pent
In narrow Room: Lims are of small Extent.
     But Thoughts are always free.
        And as they're best,
    So can they even in the Brest,
    Rove ore the World with Libertie:
    Can enter Ages, Present be
In any Kingdom, into Bosoms see.
    Thoughts, Thoughts can come to Things, and view
    What Bodies cant approach unto.
They know no Bar, Denial, Limit, Wall:
But have a Liberty to look on all.

    Like Bees they flie from Flower to Flower,
Appear in Evry Closet, Temple, Bower;
        And suck the Sweet from thence.
            No ey can see:
    As Tasters to the Deitie.
    Incredible's their Excellence.
    For ever-more they will be seen
Nor ever moulder into less Esteem.
    They ever shew an Equal face,
    And are Immortal in their place.
Ten thousand Ages hence they are as Strong,
Ten thousand Ages hence they are as Yong.

Thomas Traherne, c. 1670

An Oxford Gentleman...

Wherever philosophical insight is combined with literary genius and personal charm, one says instinctively 'That man is, or ought to be, an Oxford man.'

G. W. Russell,

WE could pass our lives in Oxford without having or wanting any other idea – that of the place is enough. We imbibe the air of thought; we stand in the presence of learning ... The enlightened and the ignorant are on a level, if they have but faith in the tutelary genius of the place. We may be wise by proxy, and studious by prescription ...

Let him then who is fond of indulging in a dreamlike existence go to Oxford, and stay there; let him study this magnificent spectacle, the same under all aspects, with its mental twilight tempering the glare of noon, or mellowing the silver moonlight; let him wander in her sylvan suburbs, or linger in her cloistered halls; but let him not catch the din of scholars or teachers, or dine or sup with them, or speak a word to any of the privileged inhabitants; for if he does, the spell will be broken, the poetry and the religion gone, and the palace of the enchantment will melt from his embrace into thin air!

William Hazlitt, 1824

'IT's a wonderful place is Oxford. You English gentlemen arrivin' here from variously located parts of the country must feel fair cowed when you think of all the famous men who have lived in this little town before you.'

No one offered to interrupt his monologue.

'You must feel a thrill in your bones when you say to yourselves, "I'm walkin' the streets which John Ruskin has walked; I am livin' on the very same ward as has once contained Arnold, Froude and Newman ..." I would give a thousand dollars,' said Downy, 'to have been up here with Newman!'

None of the undergraduates looked as if he would have given a Greek grammar for it. Only one of them showed signs of life; he cleared his throat and moved uneasily in his chair for a few moments.

'Which Newman do you mean?' he asked.

'Why, Newman, sir; the Newman.'

'Do you mean W.G.Newman who fielded point, or T.P.Newman who broke the roof of the pavilion in the M.C.C. match?'

All the freshmen glared at Downy.

'Neither, sir, neither; Cardinal Newman, the eminent divine!'

'Never heard of him!' said the bold freshman, and went on with his egg.

George Leslie Calderon, 1902

IT IS enacted that scholars of all conditions shall keep away from inns, eating-houses, wine-shops, and all houses whatever within the city, or precinct of the University, wherein wine or any other drink, or the Nicotian herb, or tobacco, is commonly sold ...

Laudian Code, 1636

Mirth is as necessary to health as are Food and Sleep.

Robert Grosseteste, 1224

Bath Place leading to the Turf Tavern

BESIDES the libraries of Radcliffe and Bodley and the Colleges, there have been of late years many libraries founded in our coffee-houses for the benefit of such as have neglected or lost their Latin or Greek ... As there are here books suited to every taste, so there are liquors adapted to every species of reading. Amorous tales may be perused over Arrack, punch and jellies; insipid odes over Orgeat or Capilaire; politics over coffee; divinity over port; and Defences of bad generals and bad ministers over Whipt Syllabubs. In a word, in these libraries instruction and pleasure go hand in hand, and we may pronounce, in a literal sense, that learning no longer remains a dry pursuit.

Thomas Warton c. 1760

Balm of my cares, sweet solace of my toils!
Hail juice benignant!

Thomas Warton

The Lamb and Flag

I rise about nine, get to breakfast by ten,
Blow a tune on my flute, or perhaps make a pen;
Read a play till eleven, or cock my lac'd hat;
Then step to my neighbours, 'till dinner, to chat.
Dinner over, to *Tom's* or to *James's* I go,
The news of the town so impatient to know;
While *Law, Locke,* and *Newton,* and all the rum race,
That talk of their modes, their ellipses, and space,
The seat of the soul, and new systems on high,
In holes, as abstruse as their mysteries, lie.
From the coffee-house then I to tennis away,
And at five I post back to my college to pray:

I sup before eight, and secure from all duns,
Undauntedly march to the *Mitre* or *Tuns*;
Where in punch or good claret my sorrows I drown,
And toss off a bowl 'To the best in town;'
At one in the morning, I call what's to pay,
Then home to my college I stagger away;
Thus I tope all the night, as I trifle all day.

Thomas Warton, 1764

Remote and ineffectual Don
That dared attack my Chesterton,
With that poor weapon, half-impelled,
Unlearnt, unsteady, hardly held,
Unworthy for a tilt with men –
Your quavering and corroded pen;
Don poor at Bed and worse at Table,
Don pinched, Don starved, Don miserable;
Don stuttering, Don with roving eyes,
Don nervous, Don of crudities;
Don clerical, Don ordinary,
Don self-absorbed and solitary;
Don here-and-there, Don epileptic;
Don middle-class, Don sycophantic,
Don dull, Don brutish, Don pedantic;
Don hypocritical, Don bad,
Don furtive, Don three-quarters mad;
Don (since a man must make an end),
Don that shall never be my friend.

Don different from those regal Dons!
With hearts of gold and lungs of bronze,
Who shout and bang and roar and bawl
The Absolute across the hall,
Or sail in amply billowing gown
Enormous through the Sacred Town,
Bearing from College to their homes
Deep cargoes of gigantic tomes;
Dons admirable! Dons of might!
Uprising on my inward sight
Compact of ancient tales, and port
And sleep – and learning of a sort.
Dons English, worthy of the land;
Dons rooted; Dons that understand.
Good dons perpetual that remain
A landmark, walling in the plain –
The horizon of my memories –
Like large and comfortable trees.

Hilaire Belloc, 1910

How these curiosities
would be quite forgott,
did not such idle fellowes
as I am, putt them down.

John Aubrey

You will find it
very good practice
always to verify
your references, sir.

Dr Routh

Never retreat.
Never explain.
Get it done
and let them howl.

Jowett

THE first time I met Colonel T.E. Lawrence ... must have been in February or March 1920, and the occasion was a guest-night at All Souls', where he had been awarded a seven-years' fellowship ... Lawrence had not long finished with the Peace Conference ... and was now tinkering at the second draft of *The Seven Pillars of Wisdom*, his fellowship having been granted him on the condition that he wrote the book as a formal history of the Arab Revolt ...

He behaved very much like an undergraduate at times. He told me of two or three schemes for brightening All Souls' and Oxford generally. One was for improving the rotten turf in the Quadrangle; he had suggested at a College meeting that it should be manured or replaced; no action was taken. He now proposed to plant mushrooms on it, so that they would be forced to returf the whole extent; and consulted a mushroom expert in town. But the technical difficulties of mushroom culture proved to be great, and Lawrence went away to help Winston Churchill with the Middle-Eastern settlement of 1922 before they could be overcome.

Another scheme, for which he enlisted my help, was to steal the Magdalen College deer. We would drive them one early morning into the small inner quadrangle of All Souls', having persuaded the College to answer the Magdalen protests with a declaration that it was the All Souls' herd, pastured there from time immemorial. Great things were expected of this raid, but we needed Lawrence as the stage-manager; so it fell through when he left us.

Robert Graves, 1929

IF Mr Rhodes's trust should be the means of our getting some gigantic Colonials ... who can do great things, say, at putting the weight, we may be able to wipe out Cambridge altogether. All Oxonians would agree that that would be a great achievement.

W. T. Stead, 1902

The Thames at Iffley

THE old scene passed before my eyes like a familiar dream, the moving crowd upon the banks, the barges loaded with ladies and their squires, the movement of small boats, canoes and skiffs darting about the river, punts crossing with their standing freights of men huddled together, then the first gun booming from Iffley, people looking at their watches, the minute gun five minutes later and last the report which started the boats and told us they were off. Then the suspense, the listening, the straining of the eyes, the first movement in the distant crowd now seen to be running, the crowd pouring over the Long Bridges, the far away shouting rising into a roar as the first boat came round the point with the light flashing upon the pinionlike motion of the rising and falling oars, the river now alive with boats, the strain and the final struggle, the plash of oars, the mad uproar, the frantic shouting as the boats pass the flag scatheless, then the slow procession following, the victors rowing proudly in amongst plaudits from the barges and the shore while the vanquished come humbly behind.

Francis Kilvert, 1876

To take your stand at the wicket in a posture of haughty defiance:
To confront a superior bowler as he confronts you:
To feel the glow of ambition, your own and that of your side:
To be aware of shapes hovering, bending, watching around — white-flannelled shapes — all eager, unable to catch you.

The unusually fine weather,

To play more steadily than a pendulum; neither hurrying nor delaying, but marking the right moment to strike.

To slog:

The utter oblivion of all but the individual energy:
The rapid co-operation of hand and eye projected into the ball;
The ball triumphantly flying through air, you too flying.
The perfect feel of a fourer!
The hurrying to and fro between the wickets: the marvellous quickness of all the fields:
The cut, leg hit, forward drive, all admirable in their way;
The pull transcending all pulls over the boundary ropes, sweeping, orotund, astral:
The superciliousness of standing still in your ground, content, and masterful, conscious of an unquestioned six;
The continuous pavilion-thunder bellowing after each true lightning stroke;
. . .

The high perpendicular puzzling hit: the consequent collision and miss: the faint praise of 'well tried.'
The hidden delight of some and the loud disappointment of others.
. . .

To have a secret misgiving:
To feel the sharp sudden rattle of the stumps from behind, electric, incredible:
To hear the short convulsive clap, announcing all is over.

The return to the pavilion, sad, and slow at first: gently breaking into
  a run amid a tumult of applause;
The doffing of the cap (without servility) in becoming acknowledgement;
The joy of what has been and the sorrow for what might have been
  mingling madly for the moment in cider-cup.
The ultimate alteration of the telegraph.

The game is over; yet for me never over:
For me it remains a memory and meaning wondrous mystical.
Bat-stroke and bird-voice (tally of my soul) 'slog, slog, slog.'
The jubilant cry from the flowering thorn to the flowerless willow,
  'smite, smite, smite.'
(Flowerless willow no more but every run a late-shed perfect bloom).
The fierce chant of my demon brother issuing forth against the demon
  bowler, 'hit him, hit him, hit him.'
The thousand melodious cracks, delicious cracks, the responsive echoes of
  my comrades and the hundred thence-resulting runs, passionately
  yearned for, never, never again to be forgotten ...

R., 1886

The Parks

OXFORD, that lotus-land, saps the will-power, the power of action. But, in doing so, it clarifies the mind, makes larger the vision, gives, above all, that playful and caressing suavity of manner which comes of a conviction that nothing matters, except ideas, and that not even ideas are worth dying for, inasmuch as the ghosts of them slain seem worthy of yet more piously elaborate homage than can be given to them in their heyday. If the colleges could be transferred to the dry and bracing top of some hill, doubtless they would be more evidently useful to the nation. But let us be glad there is no engineer or enchanter to compass that task. *Egomet*, I would liefer have the rest of England subside into the sea than have Oxford set on a salubrious level. For there is nothing in England to be matched with what lurks in the vapours of these meadows, and in the shadows of these spires — that mysterious, inenubilable spirit, spirit of Oxford. Oxford! The very sight of the word printed, or sound of it spoken, is fraught for me with most actual magic.

Max Beerbohm, 1911

And, as for me, though that my wit be lyte,
On bokes for to rede I me delyte,
And in myn herte have hem in reverence,
And to hem yeve swich lust and swich credence,
That there is wel unethe game noon,
That from my bokes make me to goon:
But hit be other upon a haly-day,
Or elles in the joly time of May;
When that I here the smale foules singe,
And that the floures ginne for to springe,
Farwell my studie, as lasting that sesoun!

Geoffrey Chaucer, c.1387

When you have wearied of the valiant spires of this County Town,
Of its wide white streets and glistening museums, and black monastic
   walls.
Of its red motors and lumbering trams, and self-sufficient people,
I will take you walking with me to a place you have not seen —
Half-town and half country — the land of the Canal ...

James Elroy Flecker, c.1907

Oxford Canal, Jericho

That halcyon time

O fortunati nimium, bona si sua norint.

O too fortunate, if only you had known how happy you were.

Clarendon

The Rainbow Bridge

All in the golden afternoon
  Full leisurely we glide:
For both our oars, with little skill,
  By little arms are plied,
While little hands make vain pretence
  Our wanderings to guide.

Ah, cruel Three! In such an hour
    Beneath such dreamy weather,
To beg a tale of breath too weak
    To stir the tiniest feather!
Yet what can one poor voice avail
    Against three tongues together?

Anon, to sudden silence won,
    In fancy they pursue
The dream-child moving through a land
    Of wonders wild and new,
In friendly chat with bird or beast
    And half believe it true.

Thus grew the tale of Wonderland:
    Thus slowly, one by one,
Its quaint events were hammered out
    And now the tale is done,
And home we steer, a merry crew,
    Beneath the setting sun.

Alice! a childish story take,
    And with a gentle hand
Lay it where Childhood's dreams are twined
    In Memory's mystic band,
Like pilgrim's wither'd wreath of flowers
    Pluck'd in a far-off land.

Lewis Carroll, 1865

I HAD sent my heroine straight down a rabbit-hole, to begin with without the least idea what was to happen afterwards ... In writing it out, I added many fresh ideas, which seemed to grow of themselves when, years afterwards, I wrote it all over again for publication. Full many a year has slipped away, since that 'golden afternoon' that gave thee birth, but I can call it up almost as clearly as if it were yesterday – the cloudless blue above, the watery mirror below, the boat drifting idly on its way, the tinkle of the drops that fell from the oars, as they waved so sleepily to and fro, and ... the three eager faces, hungry for news of fairy-land, and who would not be said 'nay' to, from whose lips 'Tell us a story, please' had all the stern immutability of Fate.

Lewis Carroll

The Lane to Old Marston

In summer fields the meadowsweet
Spreads its white bloom around the feet
Of those who pass in love or play
The golden hours of holiday:
Where heart to answering heart can beat
There grows the simple meadowsweet.   *W. L. Courtney*

To all this must be added the full song of woodland birds; the long vibrating notes of curlews, the first fresh green of deciduous trees. Year after year all this loveliness for eye and ear recurs: in early days, in youth, it was anticipated with confidence; in later years, as the season approaches, experience and age qualify the confidence with apprehension lest clouds of war or civil strife, or some emergency of work, or declining health, or some form of human ill may destroy the pleasure or even the sight of it: and when once again it has been enjoyed we have a sense of gratitude greater than in the days of confident and thoughtless youth. Perhaps the memory of those days, having become part of our being, helps us in later life to enjoy each passing season. In every May, with the same beauty of sight and sound, 'we do beget that golden time again'.

Grey of Fallodon, 1927

Shotover, once a royal forest, where John Milton's grandfather was an under-ranger.

I know each lane, and every alley green,
Dingle or bushy dell of this wild wood,
And every bosky bourn from side to side,
My daily walks and ancient neighborhood ...

John Milton, 1634

How changed is here each spot man makes or fills!
In the two Hinkseys nothing keeps the same;
The village street its haunted mansion lacks,
And from the sign is gone Sibylla's name,
And from the roofs the twisted chimney stacks –
Are ye too changed, ye hills?
See, 'tis no foot of unfamiliar men
To-night from Oxford up your pathway strays!
Here came I often, often, in old days –
Thyrsis and I; we still had Thyrsis then.

Runs it not here, the track by Childsworth Farm,
Past the high wood, to where the elm-tree crowns
The hill behind whose ridge the sunset flames?
The signal-elm, that looks on Ilsley Downs,
The Vale, the three lone weirs, the youthful Thames? –
This winter-eve is warm,
Humid the air! leafless, yet soft as spring,
The tender purple spray on copse and briers!
And that sweet city with her dreaming spires,
She needs not June for beauty's heightening.

Lovely all times she lies, lovely tonight! –
Only, methinks, some loss of habit's power
Befalls me wandering through this upland dim;
Once pass'd I blindfold here, at any hour;
Now seldom come I, since I came with him.
That single elm-tree bright
Against the west – I miss it! is it gone?
We prized it dearly; while it stood, we said,
Our friend, the Gipsy-Scholar, was not dead;
While the tree lived, he in these fields lived on.

Where is the girl, who by the boatman's door,
Above the locks, above the boating throng,
Unmoor'd our skiff when through the Wytham flats,
Red loosestrife and blond meadow-sweet among
And darting swallows and light water-gnats,

We track'd the shy Thames shore?
Where are the mowers, who, as the tiny swell
  Of our boat passing heaved the river-grass,
  Stood with suspended scythe to see us pass?
They are all gone, and thou art gone as well!

But hush, the upland hath a sudden loss
  Of quiet! – Look, adown the dusk hill-side,
  A troop of Oxford hunters going home,
As in old days, jovial and talking, ride!
  From hunting with the Berkshire hounds they come.
    Quick! let me fly, and cross
Into yon farther field! – 'Tis done; and see,
  Befalls me wandering through this upland dim,
  The orange and pale violet evening sky,
Bare on its lonely ridge, the Tree! the Tree!

Matthew Arnold, 1867

And once we rowed together up the river
To many-gated Godstow, where the stream
Splits, and upon a tongue of land there stands
An Inn with willow bowers: – it is a spot
Where still the flavour of old Merry England
Lingers: And softly flowed the silver Thames
Beside the garden, while we fed the fish.
There 'mid the ballad of Fair Rosamund:
And when at last we loosed the boat, we saw
Above the ruined Nunnery where she sleeps
A star: and from the reeds a mournful gust
Whispered and rippled round the shallow prow
And passed: and all was quiet ...

Gascoigne Mackie

The Ruins of Godstow Nunnery

ROSAMUND the fair Daughter of *Walter* Lord *Clifford*, concubine to *Henry* the second, (poysoned by *Q. Elianor*, as one thought) dying at Woodstock, where *K. Henry* had made for her an House of a wonderful working, so that no Man or Woman might come to her, but if he were instructed by the King, or such as were right secret with him touching the matter. This House after some was named *Labyrinthus*, or *Dedalus* work, which was thought to be an House wrought like unto a Knot in a Garden, called Maze, but it was commonly said, that lastly the Queen came to her by a clew of Thread, or Silk, and so dealt with her, that she lived not long after, but when she was Dead, she was buried at *Godstow*, in a House of Nunns, beside Oxford.

The Lady's Father having been a great Friend to this Nunnery, and she having spent part of her Time among the Nuns, who, during the innocent part of her Life, were mightily delighted with her Conversation (for her Parts were equal to her Beauty) no one will wonder, that after her Death, her Body was convey'd hither (especially since her self was likewise a considerable Benefactress to the Place) and bury'd in one of the chief Parts of the Church. History informs us, that it was laid in the middle of the Choir, and that there was a very handsome Tomb erected to her Memory, with very fine Lights about it, constantly burning. King *Henry* himself had also a particular Affection for the Place, as well as he had for this most accomplish'd Lady ...

John Stow, 1580

A tale begun in other days,
    When summer suns were glowing –
A simple chime, that served to time
    The rhythm of our rowing –
Whose echoes live in memory yet,
Though envious years would say 'forget.'

And though the shadow of a sigh
    May tremble through the story,
For 'happy summer days' gone by,
    And vanish'd summer glory –
It shall not touch with breath of bale
The pleasance of our fairy-tale.

Lewis Carroll, 1872

In Memoriam

I am the man who looked for peace and found
My own eyes barbed.
I am the man who groped for words and found
An arrow in my hand ...

Sidney Keyes

Noon strikes on England, noon on Oxford town,
—Beauty she was statue cold — there's blood upon her gown:
Noon of my dreams, O noon!
   Proud and godly kings had built her, long ago,
   With her towers and tombs and statues all arow,
With her fair and floral air and the love that lingers there,
   And the streets where the great men go.

James Elroy Flecker, 1914

THE outbreak of war in the year 1914 found me by chance in England, and there I remained, chiefly at Oxford, until the day of the peace. During those five years, in rambles to Iffley and Sandford, to Godstow and Wytham, to the hospitable eminence of Chilswell, to Wood Eaton or Nuneham or Abingdon or Stanton Harcourt ... these Soliloquies were composed ... Often over Port Meadow the whirr of aeroplanes sent an iron tremor through these reveries; and the daily casualty list, the constant sight of the wounded, the cadets strangely replacing the undergraduates, made the foreground to these distances ...

Skylarks, if they exist elsewhere, must be homesick for England. They need these kindly mists to hide and to sustain them. Their flexible throats would soon be parched, far from these vaporous meadows and hedgerows rich in berries and loam. How should they live in arid tablelands or at merciless altitudes, where there is nothing but scorching heat or a freezing blizzard? ... Like English poets they sing to themselves of nature, inarticulately happy in a bath of light and freedom, sporting for the sake of sport, turning what doubts they may have into sweetness, not asking to see or know anything ulterior. They must needs drink the dew amongst these English fields, peeping into the dark little hearts and flushed petals of these daisies, like the heart and cheeks of an English child, or into these buttercups, yellow like his Saxon hair. They could hardly have built their nest far from this maze of little streams, or from these narrow dykes and ditches, arched with the scented tracery of limes and willows. They needed this long, dull, chilly winter in which to gather their unsuspected fund of yearning and readiness for joy; so that when high summer comes at last they may mount with virgin confidence and ardour through these sunlit spaces, to pour their souls out at heaven's gate.

At heaven's gate, but not in heaven. The sky, as these larks rise higher and higher, grows colder and thinner; if they could rise high enough, it would be a black void. All this fluid and dazzling atmosphere is but the drapery of earth; this cerulean vault is only a film round the oceans. As these choristers pass beyond the nether veils of air, the sun becomes fierce and comfortless; they freeze and are dazzled; they must hurry home again to earth if they would live . . . but their song never comes down. Up there they leave it, in the glittering desert it once ravished, in what we call the past.

They bore their glad offering to the gate and returned empty; but the gladness of it, which in their palpitation and hurry they only half guessed, passed in and is a part of heaven. In the home of all good, from which their frail souls fetched it for a moment, it is still audible for any ear that ever again can attune itself to that measure. All that was loved or beautiful at any time, or that shall be so hereafter, all that never was but that ought to have been, lives in that paradise, in the brilliant treasure-house of the gods.

How many an English spirit, too modest to be heard here, has now committed its secret to that same heaven! Caught by the impulse of the hour, they rose like larks in the morning, cheerily, rashly, to meet the unforeseen, fatal, congenial adventure, the goal not seen, the air not measured, but the firm heart steady through the fog or blinding fire, making the best of what came, trembling but ready for what might come, with a simple courage which was half joy in living and half willingness to die. Their first flight was often their last. What fell to earth was only a poor dead body, one of a million; what remained above perhaps nothing to speak of, some boyish sally or wistful fancy, less than the song of a lark for God to treasure up in his omniscience and eternity. Yet these common brave fools knew as well as the lark the thing that they could do, and did it; and of other gifts and other adventures they were not envious. Boys and free men are always a little inclined to flout what is not the goal of their present desires, or is beyond their present scope; spontaneity in them has its ebb-flow in mockery. Their tight little selves are too vigorous and too clearly determined to brood much upon distant things; but they are true to their own nature, they know and love the sources of their own strength. Like the larks, those English boys had drunk here the quintessence of many a sunlit morning; they had rambled through these same fields, fringed with hedges and peeping copse and downs purple with heather; these paths and streams had enticed them often; they had been vaguely happy in these quiet, habitable places. It was enough for them to live, as for nature to revolve; and fate, in draining in one draught the modest cup of their spirit, spared them the weary dilution and waste of it in the world. The length of things is vanity, only their height is joy.

George Santayana, 1915

Trenches in the moonlight, allayed with lulling moonlight,
Have had their loveliness; when dancing dewy grasses
Caressed us stumping along their earthy lanes;
When the crucifix hanging over was strangely illumined,
And one imagined music, one ever heard the brave bird
In the sighing orchards flute above the weedy well.
There are such moments; forgive me that I throne them,
Nor gloze that there comes soon the nemesis of beauty,
In the fluttering relics that at first glimmer awakened
Terror — the no-man's ditch suddenly forking:
There, the enemy's best with bombs and brains and courage!
– Soft, swift, at once be animal and angel –
But O no, no, they're Death's malkins dangling in the wire
    For the moon's interpretation.

Edmund Blunden, 1928

IN October 1919, I went to Oxford at last ... We found the University remarkably quiet. The returned soldiers did not feel tempted to rag about, break windows, get drunk, or have tussles with the police and races with the Proctors' 'bulldogs', as in the old days. The boys straight from the public schools kept quiet too, having had war preached at them continually for four years, with orders to carry on loyally at home while their brothers served in the trenches, and make themselves worthy of such sacrifices. G.N. Clark, a history don at Oriel, who had got his degree at Oxford just before the war and meanwhile been an infantryman in France and a prisoner in Germany, told me: 'I can't make out my pupils at all. They are all "Yes, sir" and "No, sir". They seem positively to thirst for knowledge and scribble away in their note-books like lunatics. I can't remember a single instance of such stern endeavour in pre-war days.'

I found the English Literature course tedious, especially the insistence on eighteenth-century poets. My tutor, Percy Simpson, the editor of Ben Jonson's plays, sympathized, telling me that he had suffered once, as a boy, for preferring the Romantic Revivalists. When his schoolmaster beat him for reading Shelley, he had protested between the blows: 'Shelley is beautiful! Shelley is beautiful!' Yet he warned me not on any account to disparage the eighteenth century when I sat for my finals. I also found it difficult to concentrate on cases, genders, and irregular verbs in Anglo-Saxon grammar. The Anglo-Saxon lecturer was candid about his subject; it was, he said, a language of pure linguistic interest, and hardly a line of Anglo-Saxon poetry extant possessed the slightest literary merit. I disagreed. I thought of Beowulf lying wrapped in a blanket among his platoon of drunken thanes in the Gothland billet; Judith going for a *promenade* to Holofernes' staff-tent; and *Brunanburgh* with its bayonet-and-cosh fighting – all this came far closer to most of us than the drawing-room and deer-park atmosphere of the eighteenth century. Edmund Blunden, who also had leave to live on Boar's Hill because of gassed lungs, was taking the same course. The war still continued for both of us, and we translated everything into trench-warfare terms. In the middle of a lecture I would have a sudden very clear experience of men on the march up the Béthune-La Bassée road; the men would be singing, while French children ran along beside us, calling out: 'Tommee, Tommee, give me bullee beef!' and I would smell the stench of the knacker's yard just outside the town. Or it would be in Laventie High Street, passing a company stumps. Or in a deep dug-out at Cambrin, talking to a signaller; I would look up the shaft and see somebody's muddy legs coming down the steps; then there would be a sudden crash and the tobacco smoke in the dug-out would shake with the concussion and twist about in patterns like the marbling on books. These day-dreams persisted like an alternate life and did not leave me until well in 1928. The scenes were nearly always recollections of my first four months in France; the emotion-recording apparatus seemed to have failed after Loos.

Robert Graves, 1929

On such a morning as this
  with the birds ricocheting their music
Out of the whelming elms
  to a copper beech's embrace
And a sifting sound of leaves
  from multitudinous branches
Running across the park
  to a chequer of light on the lake,
On such a morning as this
  with *The Times* for June the eleventh
Left with coffee and toast
  you opened the breakfast-room window
And, sprawled on the southward terrace,
  said: 'That means war in September.'

Friend of my youth, you are dead!
  and the long peal pours from the steeple
Over this sunlit quad
  in our University city
And soaks in Headington stone.
  Motionless stand the pinnacles.
Under a flying sky
  as though they too listened and waited
Like me for your dear return
  with a Bullingdon noise of an evening
In a Sports-Bugatti from Thame
  that belonged to a man in Magdalen.
Friend of my youth, you are dead!
  and the quads are empty without you.

Then there were people about.
  Each hour, like an Oxford archway,
Opened on long green lawns
  and distant unvisited buildings
And you my friend were explorer
  and so you remained to me always
Humorous, reckless, loyal –
  my kind, heavy-lidded companion.

Stop, oh many bells, stop
    pouring on roses and creeper
Your unremembering peal
    this hollow, unhallowed V.E. day, –
I am deaf to your notes and dead
    by a soldier's body in Burma.

John Betjeman, 1945

At home, as in no other city, here
summer holds her breath in a dark street
the trees nocturnally scented, lovers like moths
go by silently on the footpaths
and spirits of the young wait
cannot be expelled, multiply each year.

In the meadows, walks, over the walls
the sunlight, far-travelled, tired and content,
warms the recollections of old men, touching
the hand of the scholar on his book, marching
through quadrangles and arches, at last spent
it leans through the stained windows and falls.

This then is the city of young men, of beginning,
ideas, trials, pardonable follies,
the lightness, seriousness and sorrow of youth.
And the city of the old, looking for truth,
browsing for years, the mind's seven bellies
filled, become legendary figures, seeming

stones of the city, her venerable towers;
dignified, clothed by erudition and time.
For them it is not a city but an existence;
outside which everything is a pretence:
within, the leisurely immortals dream,
venerated and spared by the ominous hours.

Keith Douglas, 1941

They are all gone into the world of light.

Henry Vaughan

The Spirit of Oxford

Fate, Time, Occasion, Chance, and Change? To these
All things are subject but eternal Love.

Shelley

The High

The stream-like windings of that glorious street

Wordsworth

At sunset or at dawn the city's place in the world, as a beautiful thing, is clearest. Few cities look other than sad at those hours . . . Oxford becomes part of the magic of sunset and dawn —, is, as it were, gathered into the bosom of the power that is abroad. Yet, if it is one with the hills and the clouds and the silence, the human dignity of the place is also significant. The work of the ancient architect conspires with that of the sunset and of long pregnant tracts of time; and I know not whether to thank, for the

Oxford from South Park

beauty of the place, its genius or perhaps the divinest series of accidents that have ever agreed to foster the forward-looking designs of men. In the days when what is admirable in Oxford was built, the builder made no pretence to please his neighbour. He made what he loved. In many cases he was probably indifferent to everything else. But the genius of the place took care; ...

... the story was told that two barefooted, hungry travellers from the west were approaching Oxford, and had come in sight of it near Cumnor, when they found a beautiful woman seated by the wayside. So beautiful was she that they knelt at her feet, 'being simple men.' ... Whereat she 'raised her small golden head so that in the sun her hair seemed to flow and flow continually down,' and looked towards Oxford. There two spires and two towers could just be seen betwixt the oak trees. 'My name,' she said, 'is known to all men save you. It is Pulchritudo. And that,' as she pointed to the shining stones of the city, 'is my home.' Those two were silent, between amazement and joy ... Hardly had they resumed their ordinary pace when they found an old man, seated by the wayside, very white and yet 'very pleasant and alluring to behold.' So to him also the simple wayfarers knelt down. Then that old man bent forward and spoke to them with golden words. 'My name is Sapienta,' he said, and 'that is my home,' he continued, and looked towards Oxford, where two spires and two towers could just be seen betwixt the oak trees. 'And,' he concluded solemnly, 'that woman is my mother and she grows not old.' The men went their way, one saying, 'It is a place of lies'; the other saying, 'It is wonderful'; and when they looked back the old man and the beautiful woman had vanished. In the city they were often seen, but the two strangers could not speak with them, 'for they were greatest in the city of Oxford.' And when they had dwelt in Oxford a short time ... the one said, 'I believe that what Sapienta and Pulchritudo said was the truth'; and the other said, 'Truly the city is worthy of them both'; wherefore they dwelt there until their deaths ...

Edward Thomas, 1903

IN Oxford nothing is the creation of one man or of one year. Every college and church and garden is the work of centuries of men and time. Many a stone reveals an octave of colour that is the composition of a long age. The founder of a college laid his plans; in part, perhaps he fixed them in stone. His successors continued the work, and without haste, without contempt of the future or ignorance of the past, helped the building to ascend unto complete beauty by means of its old and imperfect selves.

Edward Thomas, 1903

THERE are seven notes in the scale; make them fourteen, yet what a slender outfit for so vast an enterprise! What science brings so much out of so little? ... To many men the very names which the science employs are utterly incomprehensible. To speak of an idea or subject seems to be fanciful or trifling; to speak of the views which it opens upon us to be childish extravagance; yet is it possible that that inexhaustible evolution and disposition of notes, so rich, yet so simple, so intricate, yet so regulated, so various, yet so majestic, should be a mere sound which is gone and perishes? Can it be that these mysterious stirrings of heart and keen emotions, and strange yearnings after we know not what, and awful impressions from we know not whence, should be wrought in us by what is unsubstantial, and comes and goes, and begins and ends in itself? It is not so; it cannot be. No; they have escaped from some higher sphere; they are the outpourings of eternal harmony in the medium of created sound ...

John Henry Newman

New College Cloisters

Who shaped these walls, has shewn
The music of his mind,
Made known, though thick through stone
What beauty beat behind ...

Who built these walls made known
The music of his mind,
Yet here he has but shewn
His ruder-rounded rind.
His brightest blooms lie there unblown,
His sweetest nectar hides behind.

Gerard Manley Hopkins, c.1876

Looking down Brasenose Lane

Know you her secret none can utter?
   Her of the Book, the tripled Crown?
Still on the spire the pigeons flutter
   Still by the gateway flits the gown:
Still in the street, from corbel and gutter
   Faces of stone look down.

Once, my dear — but the world was young then —
   Magdalen elms and Trinity limes —
Lissom the oars and backs that swung then,
   Eight good men in the good old times —
Careless we and the chorus flung then
   Under St. Mary's chimes!

Come, old limmer, the times grow colder;
   Leaves of the creeper redden and fall,
Was it a hand, then, clapped my shoulder?
   — Only the wind by the chapel wall ...

Still on her spire the pigeons hover;
   Still by her gateway haunts the gown;
Ah, but her secret? you, young lover,
   Drumming her old ones forth from town,
Know you the secret none discover?
   Tell it when *you* go down.

Yet if at length you seek her, prove her,
   Lean to her whispers never so nigh;
Yet if at last not less her lover
   You in your hansom leave the High;
Down from her towers a ray shall hover —
   Touch you, a passer-by.

                              A. T. Quiller-Couch, 1896

He gave man speech, and speech created thought,
Which is a measure of the universe.

Shelley

THERE must be such a thing as *Religio Grammatici*, the special religion of a 'Man of Letters.'

The greater part of life is rigidly confined in the round of things that happen from hour to hour ... Man is imprisoned in the external present; and what we call a man's religion is, to a great extent, the thing that offers him a secret and permanent means of escape from that prison, a breaking of the prison walls which leaves him standing, of course, still in the present, but in a present so enlarged and enfranchised that it is become not a prison but a free world ...

And men find it, of course, in a thousand ways, with different degrees of ease and certainty ... Some find it in theology, some in art, in human affection; in the anodyne of constant work; in that permanent exercise of the inquiring intellect which is commonly called the search for Truth; some find it in carefully cultivated illusions of one sort or another, in passionate faiths and undying pugnacities; some, I believe, find a substitute by simply rejoicing in their prison, and living furiously, for good or ill, in the actual moment.

And a Scholar, I think, secures his freedom by keeping hold always of the past and treasuring up the best out of the past, so that in a present that may be angry or sordid he can call back memories of calm or of high passion, in a present that requires resignation or courage he can call back the spirit with which brave men long ago faced the same evils. He draws out of the past high thoughts and great emotions; he also draws the strength that comes from communion or brotherhood ...

The true *Grammaticus*, while expressing faithfully his personal predilections or special sensitivenesses, will stand in the midst of the *Grammata*, not as a captious critic, nor yet as a jealous seller of rival wares, but as a returned traveller amid the country and landscape that he loves. He will realize the amount of love and care which has gone to the making of the *Traditio*, the handing down of the intellectual acquisitions of the human race from one generation to another, the constant selection of thoughts and discoveries and feelings and events so precious that they must be made into books, and then of books so precious that they must be copied and recopied and not allowed to die. The *Traditio* itself is a wonderful and august process, full no doubt of abysmal gaps and faults, like all things human, but full also of that strange half baffled and yet not wholly baffled splendour which marks the characteristic works of man. I think the *Grammaticus*, while not sacrificing his judgement, should accept the *Traditio* and rejoice in it, rejoice to be the intellectual child of his great forefathers, to catch at their spirit, to carry on their work, to live and die for the great unknown purpose which the eternal spirit of man seems to be working out upon the earth. He will work under the guidance of love and faith; not, as so many do, under that of ennui and irritation.

My subject to-day has been the faith of a scholar, *Religio Grammatici*. This does not mean any denial or disrespect towards the religions of others. A *Grammaticus* who cannot understand other people's minds is failing in an essential part of his work. The religion of those who follow physical science is a magnificent and life-giving thing. The *Traditio* would be utterly wrecked without it. It also gives man an escape from the world about him, an escape from the noisy present into a region of facts which are as they are and not as foolish human beings want them to be; an escape from the commonness of daily happenings into the remote world of high and severely trained imagination; an escape from mortality in the service of a growing and durable purpose, the progressive discovery of truth. I can understand also the religion of the artist, the religion of the philanthropist. I can understand the religion of those many people, mostly young, who reject alike books and microscopes and easels and committees, and live rejoicing in an actual concrete present which they can ennoble by merely loving it. And the religion of Democracy? That is just what I am preaching throughout this discourse. For the cardinal doctrine of that religion is the right of every human soul to enter, unhindered except by the limitation of its own powers and desires, into the full spiritual heritage of the race.

All these things are good, and those who pursue them may well be soldiers in one army or pilgrims on the same eternal quest. If we fret and argue and fight one another now, it is mainly because we are so much under the power of the enemy. I sometimes wish that we men of science and letters could all be bound by some vow of renunciation or poverty, like monks of the Middle Ages; but of course no renunciation could be so all-embracing as really to save us from that power. The enemy has no definite name, though in a certain degree we all know him. He who puts always the body before the spirit, the dead before the living, ... who makes things only in order to sell them; who has forgotten that there is such a thing as truth, and measures the world by advertisement or by money; who daily defiles the beauty that surrounds him and makes vulgar the tragedy; whose innermost religion is the worship of the Lie in his Soul. The Philistine, the vulgarian, the Great Sophist, the passer of base coin for true, he is all about us and, worse, he has his outposts inside us, persecuting our peace, spoiling our sight, confusing our values, making a man's self seem greater than the race and the present thing more important than the eternal. From him and his influence we find our escape by means of the *Grammata* into that calm world of theirs, where stridency and clamour are forgotten in the ancient stillness, and that which was in its essence material and transitory has for the most part perished, while the things of the spirit still shine like stars. Not only the great things are there, seeming to stand out the greater because of their loneliness; there is room also for many that were once in themselves quite little, but now through the *Grammata* have acquired a magic poignancy, echoes of old tenderness or striving or laughter beckoning across gulfs of death and change; the watchwords that our dead leaders and forefathers loved, *viva adhuc et desiderio pulchriora.* 'Living still and more beautiful because of our longing.'

Gilbert Murray, 1918

Oxford from Boar's Hill

AND yet, steeped in sentiment as she lies, spreading her gardens to the moonlight, and whispering from her towers the last enchantments of the Middle Age, who will deny that Oxford, by her ineffable charm, keeps ever calling us nearer to the true goal of all of us, to the ideal, to perfection – to beauty in a word, which is only truth seen from another side . . .

Matthew Arnold

Index

The index contains not only the authors of the passages quoted, but also persons mentioned in the text. The former are distinguished by a bold page number. The bold numeral is also used to signify an illustration of a college as distinct from a reference to it in the text. Bibliographical references are given last.